# ENDNOTES FROM A *Happy Old Lady*

Rita Weber

ISBN 979-8-89785-428-8 (paperback)
ISBN 979-8-89785-429-5 (digital)



Christian Faith Publishing
Meadville, PA
www.christianfaithpublishing.com

Printed in the United States of America

# *Giving Thanks*

I SUPPOSE THERE ARE BOOKS THAT HAVE been published through the years without any acknowledgement of gratitude to a Divine Being or an expert or a trusted friend or an encourager or a helper of some kind, but not many. I mean, someone has to cook and clean, keep the wolf from the door, and entertain the kids while the writing is ongoing.

I certainly could not have written this book, as brief as it is, without lots of people being helpfully involved, and, particularly, without the Creator and Keeper of the Universe, and Savior of my soul. The inspiration of the Holy Spirit was the continual impetus that brought *End Notes of a Happy Old Lady* out of my brain and onto paper. This realization was made evident to me as I sat down in front of a laptop, put my hands on the keyboard, and watched as words appeared that often surprised me! It was like reading material that someone else was writing on the screen. Even stranger, I realized that when I was writing about difficult or painful periods in my life, I was learning things, especially spiritual things about myself, that I had previously not known or understood. I suppose there might be several explanations about such experiences, but I, being 80 years old and firm (hidebound?) in my convictions and my history with my Lord, believe these experiences were evidence of the action of the Holy Spirit in my life.

I will explain this earlier in the book, so I won't elaborate here. It is enough for me to say that my greatest and most profound thanks go to my great and gracious God, who has blessed me and taught me and led me and held me and saved me from myself for all my life. He is all that is precious and vital and real to me, and He provides all my needs from His riches in glory. Every bit of love, joy, and peace I have ever experienced in my long life has come from my loving Father, and I owe Him everything I am and have for all of eternity.

I also owe great depths of thanks to the many people in my life who, while I have been writing, have prayed for me, encouraged me, and, especially, helped me think through thorny spiritual issues that were tying me in knots and preventing me from honoring the Lord as I desperately wanted to do.

There are many names I could mention, names of people I greatly admire and even love, but I decided early on in the writing process not to cite names, lest I might unintentionally embarrass or hurt someone I respect and care for. But, there is one person that I love and esteem, who knows me well enough to know I am sometimes prone to put my foot in my mouth, or allow my whacked out sense of humor to get the best of me, and, indeed, has been subject to such treatment all her life, and has continually forgiven me. This very gracious person is my daughter, Emily, who has the sometimes dubious honor of being my best friend, and, also, fortunately for me, has a Master's Degree in English, excellent writing and copy editing skills, is a voracious reader, and, best of all, in my estimation, is a pro in my weakest area of all, the computer. Emily says that I do not speak computerese, and, yes, that is an actual word, and, yes, she is absolutely correct. But, in my own defense, I was born in a prior century. This book would absolutely not exist if it were not for Emily. She has fixed things I've messed up, found things I thought were lost forever in cyberspace, talked me down from the edge of the cliff when I reached the end of my computer rope, and brought me warm milk and sedatives when I've gone around the bend. Not that she is always calm about it. Her most frequently asked question seems to be, "How did you do this?" I never know; if I did, I might be able to fix it myself! Anyway, thank you, Emily Kathryne Weber for your (usual) good humor and (usual) patience with my computer messes, and for reading and catching errors of all sorts, from grammar to meaning, spelling to punctuation, and everything in between. ("Are you sure you want to say this, Mom?")

# *Prologue*

AROUND A YEAR AGO, A VERY GOOD friend came to visit, and soon after we were settled down with our hot beverages, she vaulted over the commonplace subjects of conversation and went straight to the spiritual interchanges we love to engage in together. I don't know how she came up with the question she asked me, except by divine prompting, but she said, apropos of nothing, "So how's your life going?" That's a pretty broad topic, and I was stumbling around, trying to put my thoughts and feelings into words, and not doing it very clearly, when my friend suddenly said, "So you're just a happy old lady."

It wasn't a question, but more of an affirmation, and my response was quick: "Exactly!" I had never verbalized it, hadn't even thought about it much, but like the first time I ever saw a real elephant, I recognized it instantly.

I am a happy old lady! What a discovery! And what a wonderful idea to take apart, examine, think about, and discover its source. I knew right away that my general state of happiness, which in my mind has a definition of peace, love, and joy, and is summed up by the promise of abundant life found in John 10:9–10, when Jesus says,

> I am the door; if anyone enters through Me, he will be saved, and will

> go in and out and find pasture. The thief comes only to steal and kill and destroy; I came that they may have life, and have it abundantly.

Anyone who has ever had the great pleasure of watching lambs frolic in a pasture has seen the illustration of joy, as the little creatures jump up in the air, kick their legs up, land with all four feet in the same spot, run to a different spot, and do it all over again. There is no reason other than sheer exuberance—pure joy! Then as they begin to tire, the little creatures go in search of their mothers for a fuel refill and lie down near them for a rest, before starting the process all over again.

I no longer engage in jumping and kicking my legs up, needing to limit my ER trips to the more serious issues that diabetes all too frequently brings on. But I have found that joy can always abound in my heart and mind, whether in my chair at home, driving in traffic, or anywhere else, for that matter—even in ERs and ICUs. Thankfully, the peace that the Lord gives is not at all dependent on what circumstances I am facing. The peace that He gives is tender but not at all fragile. It is quite resilient, in fact, and quickly replenished by a look at the One who is our peace, our Lord Jesus. Peace is also quite companionable, walking hand in hand with either joy or grief and greatly enhancing both.

There was a time in my life when I looked with scorn at the concept of being a sheep, as the Scripture refers to humankind frequently. "All we like sheep have gone astray," is sadly quite accurate. A classmate of mine in Bible school was from Iceland, and she gave a talk on her country that included the economic importance of sheep to the Icelandic economy. Her remarks about sheep included the comment that they were stupid! But years before that, when I was a freshman at the University of New Mexico, I, in many ways, rivaled sheep in stupidity, complicated by arrogance! Oh, the folly of a little bit of knowledge! Our church had, at that time, a pastor who called himself the under-shepherd and the congregation his sheep. Oh, how I resented that!

One Sunday, on the way home from church, my mother said to me, "Rita Carol (oops, I was in trouble!), if you can't do something about your face, you need to stop singing in the choir. Every person in the congregation knows exactly what you are thinking while the pastor is preaching!" I spent the rest of that year steadfastly looking down at my lap during church. I say this to illustrate that I didn't make it easy to live in the goodness of God, as the song says. It was a long time later that I finally realized that, while sheep aren't very high on the domestic animal intelligence scale, they at least know they need a shepherd, and once they find a faithful one, they will follow him anywhere. I didn't know that I needed the Shepherd when I was young and dumb and proud, and it took some pretty extreme events in my life before I figured it out. And it took even longer for me to realize that I was living in the goodness of God all that time. I didn't deserve His goodness, but He gave it to me out of His own love, mercy, and compassion. It had nothing to do with my worthiness.

Being of sound mind and body, or at least things being as good as they are likely ever to be, considering my age and ailments, I have begun thinking of my memorial service, which will be much more interesting than my last will and testament, since my worldly goods will consist largely of things my children will have to deal with the disposal thereof, rather than divvy up. The only fights will be over who has to take the next load to the local dump, and the only real legacy

I am likely to have I hold in my heart and mind. Hence, this book.

I have a file on my desk entitled *Gone to Glory*, and I have told my daughter, Emily, with whom I live, that everything she and her brother, Mark, will need to know when I get promoted to glory is to be found in that file. I don't want to have a traditional funeral. I will be cremated; my ashes mixed with my husband's (perhaps in a Tupperware bowl with a tight-fitting lid?) and sprinkled wherever the kids deem appropriate or used as mulch for my beloved garden. So funeral, no. Memorial service, yes. I've always wanted to have the last word. Ask my husband. The only way he ever got the last word was to die before me! Actually, I will leave the service planning to our children. They know my heart and that I want my last expressions on earth to be all about the goodness of God in my life and in every person's life. God loves His human creatures, made in His image, and desires that they come to know and love Him. What better use of a memorial service than those for last words! My only specific request for my memorial service is that it begin and end with the song "Goodness of God." For me, this song says all I need to say about my life.

The Holy Scripture is replete with verses about the goodness of God to His children, and even to those who don't know Him at all. There are many *common*, meaning widespread or general, blessings in the world that all of humankind can appreciate and enjoy. Things like loving marital relationships, beloved children, good food to eat, rain falling in times of drought, cool breezes on a hot day, a job one loves, and many others that some do not recognize or acknowledge as coming from a generous and caring

God. Jesus, in His teaching recorded in Matthew 5:43–45, addresses this generosity of our good God:

> You have heard that it was said, You shall love your neighbor and hate your enemy. But I say to you, love your enemies and pray for those who persecute you, so that you may be sons of your Father who is in heaven; for He causes His sun to shine on the evil and the good, and sends rain on the righteous and the unrighteous.

God's goodness is His grace, His mercy, His compassion, His favor, His blessings, the good plan He has for every person's life, and all the gifts of love that He gives to His children in greatest measure. God's goodness is also seen in times He stops us from doing things that are harmful to us or to others through us. He is a good Father, but not an indulgent One. He has a purpose for each one He creates, and He is faithful to see that good purpose fulfilled in our lives and works in many and diverse ways to make that fulfillment possible.

I believe and rejoice that everything God made me to be, everything He poured into me since even before my birth, every gene on every chromosome, every person I've encountered, every place I've been, everything I've done, every emotion, from pure joy to the depths of grief, I've experienced, all the love I've received—literally everything—has been ordained by God to shape me into the person He created me to be. I have not always enjoyed what God was doing in my life, and there were times I was angry and resentful about what was happening. But, in every instance, eventually, I worked as a clinical microbiologist in various labs, and all the while, I was attending church and learning, then teaching, the Bible.

I had a great head knowledge of God and, as I see it now, a deal, rather than a relationship, with Him. My deal, no less real for being unconscious, was along these lines: "Yay, I'm saved! I get to go to heaven when I die. In the meantime, I'll try to stay out of trouble so God won't be mad at me, and I'll call Him if I ever need help. See you at the Pearly Gates, God." And, Father, forgive me, that worked pretty well for me for almost twenty years, as I grew up, did well at school, got an interesting job, got married, had a pretty trouble-free life of marriage, working, putting my husband, Joe, through college, and, at last, having the baby we so desperately wanted.

Joe got his dream job, flying a Learjet for an oil company, and I quit my job chasing bugs in a clinical lab to stay at home with Emily, our beautiful daughter, in our recently purchased house in the country. In the interest of an accurate account, let me say that our house in the country was exactly that, a house out in the country. It was not a mansion or even a big house. There were two bedrooms, and one of them was a converted back porch, and one bath. The house was about one hundred years old, built of limestone rock with no insulation. The garage was detached and far enough away from the house to ensure a good drenching in rainy weather. The plumbing turned out to be not a septic system but a cesspool, which we found out when the tank backed up and overflowed, requiring that we destroy the back patio to find it and fix it. The furnace was in the attic, accessible only by climbing a ladder outside and going into a window, whenever the pilot light went out, which was whenever the wind blew from the north. I found this out when I was pregnant with Emily, and Joe was somewhere on the East Coast. But the acre-sized lot was beautiful, there was a small greenhouse, and a huge, beautiful oak tree in the front yard. Joe and I fell in love with the place. My ever-practical father, upon seeing the house for the first time after we bought it, walked around inside and out, and finally said, "So...you bought a tree and a house came with it." But buying a house was the next step in our dream plan, and our first baby was on the way. We were in domestic heaven.

Eighteen months after Emily's birth, my carefree, according-to-plan life suddenly stopped, and my relationship with the Savior of the world and Creator of the universe began to change from "All is well, see You later," to "God! What's happening?" The first thing that happened was that, right in the middle of my dream life, I became totally miserable. As I later learned, but sure didn't know then, misery is a tool of God, and one of the most effective tools at that.

Suddenly, I was no longer a microbiologist. I was a stay-at-home mom, out in the country with a new baby and a husband who was literally flying all over the world, and routinely gone from Sunday afternoon until Friday night. Who knew my identity had been my job? Who knew I now saw myself as a nobody? God, of course, and He was doing some divine engineering. Being miserable, and clueless on top of it, I looked around for someone to blame and quickly settled on my hapless husband, who was having the time of his life while I was living not in hell, but pretty close, even if it was a self-constructed one. Poor Joe. I began to rock his boat, the Good Ship Perfect Life. I was, as my mother often told me not to do, acting ugly, and I almost uglied my way into a divorce before I received what I eventually saw as a divine flash of insight.

One awful day, I prayed this prayer, and I still shudder at the memory. "God, I am horrible! I am useless as I am. Either change me or take me out! Amen." Less than two awful months later, I was at MD Anderson Cancer Center in Houston, having surgery for a Level 4 melanoma, with a prognosis of an 80 percent chance of dying and a 20 percent chance of living. And I knew exactly why it was happening.

I knew the instant, my gynecologist, during a routine visit, had seen a mole on the back of my arm and said, "You need to see a dermatologist today!" and had hurried off to make an appointment with a friend of his for that very afternoon.

As I watched my doctor rush out of the room, I said, "Lord, this is how You are going to change me!"

That was the beginning of my real relationship with the Lord, a relationship where we both talked, and we both responded. I saw that He was the most vital part of my life, the most important person in the world to me. My life no longer revolved around me because God had become the center of my life. And the more I knew Him, the more grateful I became for what had happened to me. Even if I died, as all my doctors expected me to, it was worth it. (I had a dermatologist tell me just last year, "Wow, Somebody up there likes you!" "Why?" said I. After all, it was forty-eight years ago since I had that first surgery. "Because you should be dead!")

Praise God that He didn't think I should be dead. The Scripture says that all the days of my life were written in the Lord's book of life even before there was yet one of them (Psalm 139:16). I will die when my appointment time comes up, and not an instant before. Hallelujah, what a blessed way to live!

Into the valley of the shadow with Him: It is a sad but true observation among Christians that while all sorts of delightful things come from our mountaintop experiences, true spiritual growth happens in the valley of the shadow. From 1976, when I had my first bout with cancer, until 1998, when Joe had his final one, we were pretty much permanent students in God's School of Getting to Know Him Through Adversity.

One of our very good friends once remarked, "Every family has something. The Webers have cancer." Joe was diagnosed with multiple myeloma, "a uniformly fatal form of blood cancer," in 1984, and given a prognosis of three years to live. Emily was nine years old then, and our son, Mark, was five. I had surgery for melanoma in 1976 and 1980, both times when our babies were eighteen months old. Pregnancy hormone-stimulated, the doctors said. So we had no more babies, being very grateful for the two we had, and I had no more cancer. Instead of just three more years, the Lord gave Joe what we called "Hezekiah's 15," though it was actually closer to fourteen years, and Joe was promoted to glory in December of 1998, when the kids were twenty-three and nineteen.

Joe was in remission for ten years, from 1984 until 1994, and I was cancer-free from 1980 forward. The shadow of the valley of death hung over us from our grim prognoses, with regular checkups a frequent reminder, but by then, forced, thankfully, into knowing the Lord much better, we knew there was a *plan*, and we were in it. As a result of that, we could live our lives in a blessed and peaceful state of mind. We built our dream home next door to my parents in Boerne, a lovely Texas Hill Country town, and went on with our lives. Joe flew corporate jets and, eventually, became the aviation director for the oil company he worked for. I was a busy mom, homeschooling two growing kids, and got a new identity as a church lady. That was still the wrong identity, but at least, I was heading in the right direction!

Easter Sunday, 1994, our extended family gathered at my youngest sister and her husband's home for lunch after church, followed by an Easter egg hunt and games with the kids in the big field next to their home. Joe was playing with the gang of kids who were running around the field when he stepped into a hole, fell to the ground, and could not get up. He had severe pain in his hip joint, such that we thought he had broken it. The ensuing trip to the emergency room was the beginning of the downward spiral that, four years later, led to Joe's death from multiple myeloma. X-rays revealed a disease process of bone destruction from the multiple lesions in the bone marrow that are typical of this blood cancer. Joe began treatment with his oncologist, recovered from his hip injury, and life went on as it had been for about two years before more extreme treatment was necessary.

During this time, the company Joe worked for was taken over by another company whose leadership believed that aviation departments were an unnecessary and wasteful expense. All the corporate jets were sold off, and the department closed. All the pilots were laid off, except for Joe, who, as department director, was kept on to sell the aircraft and supporting equipment. This took almost a year and was a very sad time for Joe.

We could see the handwriting on the wall of our future and made the very difficult decision to sell our beloved home where we had lived for seventeen years. It was a lovely house in a nice neighborhood and sold quickly. The day we left the house for the last time, Joe and I and our two children, almost adults now, stood on the big front porch and cried. The sale of our home marked the end of many things and the beginning of many more, none of them welcome. We rented a house in Boerne, which all of us hated, a feeling engendered much more by our grief over the forced change than by the rent house itself. We lived there for about two years. Joe finished up his work for the oil company, and his position was terminated. But due to his reputation in the aviation community in San Antonio, he was able to fly for several other companies in the area. One interesting job was as a test pilot for a new business jet that was being developed. Our son, Mark, when he heard about it, exclaimed, "My dad is a crash dummy!" It was good to have something to laugh at.

Eventually and inevitably, Joe's cancer picked up speed and power, and he could no longer fly because of federal regulations. He began looking for some other job to keep us afloat. I was working part-time for a real estate company by then, writing advertising copy, but it didn't make ends meet, even with our efforts to move our *ends*. About this time, our church needed a full-time janitor, and Joe applied and got the job. We were grateful to have it, and I was prouder of Joe for being willing to clean the bathrooms at our church than I ever was that he flew Learjets for a living. His cheerful humility was a great testimony to our fellow church members, friends, and family.

A lovely elderly widow at our church approached us one Sunday and said that a house she had owned and sold nearly twenty years before had come back to her because the family that bought it had just walked out on the mortgage without any attempt to sell it or make any arrangements to keep it. Mrs. M. offered to rent us that house outside of Boerne for a very low amount. We moved again, into the house where Joe eventually died. Not very long after we moved in, Mrs. M. offered to sell us the house if we would pay the closing costs and pick up the payments, which were the same amount she had been charging us for rent. She was God's provision for us, and we were thankful. The house needed work, but it was comfortable and, as a huge bonus, was out in the country on eight acres. Joe, being an Indiana farm boy at heart, was ecstatic.

I went back to work at a hospital in San Antonio, in the microbiology department, for about a year before the next chapter of our life with multiple myeloma opened. In 1996 the disease progressed to the point of requiring more extensive treatment, and a bone marrow transplant was called for. We chose to travel to Zion, Illinois, Cancer Treatment Centers of America, for the procedure, mainly because of their holistic approach to cancer treatment, emphasizing nutritional and spiritual care along with cutting-edge medical care. Our experience with this remarkable hospital was wonderful. It was everything that it should be, except that, in the end, Joe died. But, to be fair, at that time, multiple myeloma was considered a *uniformly fatal cancer*, and we had known that from the beginning.

During the year that we traveled back and forth for Joe to be treated there, he had chemotherapy to kill all the cells in his bone marrow, and two bone marrow transplants using his own stem cells to, hopefully, eradicate the cancer from his body. For a while, it seemed to have worked, and Joe felt good and got a job flying for a local company again. He and I went on a long camping trip to New Mexico in the fall, and Christmas was very, very merry. Our Sunday school class rejoiced with us. We were so thankful to the Lord for His gift of health to Joe.

Early in 1997, Joe began to show symptoms of the return of his cancer. We returned to Zion, Illinois, to the hospital, where Joe had more tests and visited with his doctor. His bone marrow transplant had failed, and the cancer cells in his marrow had begun to proliferate once more. There was nothing further that could be done, except for radiation treatments to knock back the tumors as they occurred. We returned home to an uncertain future.

Over the course of 1997 and for most of 1998, we lived in day-tight compartments, not looking to a future Joe did not have. Soon, Joe could no longer fly, and we were without income again. He went on disability status, and as a minor, our son, Mark, also received a monthly check. A group of men from our church and community, whose names we never knew, began to furnish support and continued to do so until Joe's death in late 1998. I was working for the Boerne Public Library, and the director was very considerate of our situation. We were grateful for God's faithful care, expressed through the many people who gathered around us to help in that difficult time.

I don't know how many radiation treatments Joe received in 1997 and 1998, but we joked that he glowed in the dark! They kept him going and relatively pain-free. Joe had been a Boy Scout leader for years and was able to take his troop to Philmont Scout Ranch in northern New Mexico in the fall of 1997. I don't know how he did it, hiking in mountainous terrain, carrying a seventy-pound pack, and sleeping on the ground in a tent, in cold temperatures. It was a last gift to Mark, and Joe was determined to make the trip. He came home, exhausted and in pain, but grateful for having been able to do it.

In the fall of 1998, Joe made the decision not to have any more radiation treatments. He told me of his desire to stop them and said to me, "Is that okay with you?" Those were his simple words, but there were thirty-three years of a happy, loving marriage behind them. I, of course, said yes, that he needed to do whatever he needed to do. And that was that. But inwardly, my heart was breaking. It was certainly not okay.

Things progressed quickly after that conversation. Our bedroom was upstairs, and the stairs were becoming more difficult for Joe with each day that passed. On one of our last days in our upstairs room, we were resting on our bed and listening to music on a CD player. Joe was close behind me with his arm around me when the song "Time to Say Goodbye" began to play. I tried not to cry, not wanting to upset Joe, who was being very quiet. But suddenly, I felt his tears running down the back of my neck. Not a word was said, no sound was made. That was the closest we ever came to saying goodbye and how we felt about his death.

Without radiation to knock them back, the tumors began to grow very rapidly, and within about two weeks, Joe was bedfast, hospice was engaged, and I had told my boss at the library I needed to take a leave of absence. We set up his hospital bed, facing east out a big window in a downstairs room, with my bed snugged up to his, so we could still sleep close. The days were long and tiring, but each moment was precious. We lived in the moment, taking no thought for the morrow, as it says in Matthew 6:34, just one day at a time. We watched the sun rise each morning, drinking coffee and talking about anything but what we were doing there. Really it was a time of peace and gratitude and of restful waiting. Only once did Joe speak of his impending death. We were sitting close together on his bed when he put his arms around me and said, "This will be the hardest thing you have ever done, but you will get through it. I know you will." He held me through my tears and sobs until I finally stopped, and nothing more was ever said about it.

We had fought so hard for four years, and now, there was nothing more to do. Emily and Mark were in and out from next door; friends came to visit and say goodbye. Our church choir came one evening; filling the room and down the hall, they sang hymns for Joe. The hospice nurses came every day, and they were marvelous at keeping Joe pain-free and comfortable. Enough cannot be said about the hospice care nurses. They made it possible for Joe to die at home, right where he wanted to be, and they became our good friends.

For years, Joe had been meeting weekly with a special group of men who talked and prayed and laughed together, as they supported and encouraged each other. Joe's Guys, as we called them, were very much with us during these days. Some days, one or more of them would come and sit with Joe so I could grocery shop and do other necessary things, like regain my balance and restore my serenity, as the Lord and I went up and down the aisles at the store. One of the Guys built a ramp from our front porch to the ground because he knew that Joe was anxious about not being able to get down the steps in his wheelchair. He built it just to make Joe feel better, knowing that Joe would never leave his house again. Another of the Guys was a high-level corporate executive who traveled all the time. He suspended his travel schedule to be with Joe in his last days.

The Guys each came alone to say goodbye to Joe, express love and appreciation to each other, and even laugh at good times in the past. These men had supported Joe through the toughest years in many ways, and they were faithful now at the end. Their wives were my good friends and support group and were also near at this time.

And now, twenty-five years later, these women are still my best friends, meeting weekly for coffee and laughter and tears. Two more are widows now, and all of us are either eighty or pushing it. I hope they get to see me off when I depart.

Joe never wavered in his faith and gratitude to the Lord. One day, toward the end of his earthly life, he said, "Just because I don't know the reason God does what He does doesn't mean there isn't one. And whatever God's reason for doing whatever He does is good enough for me."

We didn't talk about what was happening to him. Joe was never much of a talker, about feelings anyway, and as the cancer cells took up more space in his bone marrow, and fewer red blood cells were made, Joe's oxygen levels dropped, and his organs began to fail, including his brain.

We had put a TV in his room, but toward the end, he couldn't use the remote control. Emily came out of the room in tears one day, and when I asked her what the matter was, she said, "Mama, Daddy flew Learjets, and now he can't change the channel on the TV!" Odd, the little things that can push you over the edge sometimes.

Our last conversation, if five short sentences can be called a conversation, was, "Please pick me up! My back is so tired of lying in this bed."

I said, "Oh, honey, I can't pick you up. Only Jesus can pick you up now."

"Come on, Jesus!" were his last words before he stopped talking completely.

He slept more and more until he just stopped waking up at all. He was still breathing and seemed quite comfortable, and would rouse slightly when the nurses checked on him, but only for a few seconds.

We were just waiting. Neither I nor the hospice nurses could understand how Joe was still breathing, why he was still living. It was a quiet period, all the medical interventions completed, the goodbyes said; there was nothing to do but watch and wait.

Early in the morning of December 1, 1998, I woke and went outside to see the starry sky, crystal clear, familiar, and beautiful. I stood and watched until the cold seeped in through my clothes and I began to shiver. Returning to our house, I went into that holy space where Joe waited between the realms of here and there.

I stood by his bed and told him about the beautiful, clear sky, his *office*, as he had always called it, and how it was going to be a glorious day for a *final departure*—pilot talk for time to take off. I told him it was okay for him to leave, that the kids and I would be okay, and that God would take care of us. What a strange and flexible word *okay* is. It can have two completely different meanings at the same time, be true and untrue, and convey nothing and yet a whole world at once.

Joe showed no sign of having heard me, but he must have, because in just a little while, the sound of his breathing, which had filled the room for weeks, simply stopped. I guess he did not want me to see him leave because he waited until I had walked out of the room to escape his body and make his final departure. It sounds odd, but I heard the sudden silence. I stepped back into the room, and it was empty. Joe was not there. What still lay in the hospital bed was not Joe, and I felt no need to touch the empty shell.

Two of Joe's Guys came, arriving before the funeral home personnel. They washed Joe and dressed him in clean pajamas. And when the funeral home did arrive, the gurney they brought would not fit in the hallway to the room where Joe's body was resting. One of Joe's friends picked him up and carried him out to the gurney.

The man I had loved since I was fifteen years old and had been married to for thirty-two years was gone. I knew where he was, that he was no longer sick, and that he was at that moment in the embrace of the Lord he had loved and served for so long. That knowledge, at least right then, brought no comfort.

A curious feeling of numbness settled over me, a self-containment, a closing in, that was to protect my feelings and keep them safely inside except when I was alone with God and could pour them out in tears of grief and loneliness. I was bereft, a word I had only read but never used until then, and certainly not understood or felt. It seemed like my life had suddenly split between Then with Joe and Now without Joe.

Maybe it was a shock. I don't know. But whatever it was, it lasted a long time. I couldn't, and can't, remember anything. If it had not been for my friends and my daughter, the funeral would have been stark indeed because I did nothing to make it happen. I don't know who dealt with the church or the funeral home. There were pictures of Joe at the church. I don't know how they got there. There was a reception. I don't know who arranged it. And I don't remember any of the days that immediately followed Joe's death. I only know what I saw in photos later. There are no memories at all.

I went back to work at the library. I was cataloging new books, and I was able to do it only because it required so much concentration that I had to be focused to do it, so maybe I came out of my fog just for those eight hours a day. I didn't cry at work.

But as soon as I got in the car and headed for home, I began to cry and would cry all the way home. I got pulled over by a policewoman on the way home one day. I was doing ninety miles an hour and didn't even realize it. The kind officer could see I was crying and tried to help me. She really didn't want to give me a ticket.

But I wanted her to give me a ticket! I could have killed someone! I could have killed myself. It was an expensive lesson. During that same time period, I backed out of the garage without opening the garage door. That was expensive too.

There is a diagnosis code used by psychiatrists for acute grief. It is considered a kind of temporary insanity. There are different codes for simple grief and complicated grief. I don't know the definitions that make the difference. But the temporary insanity thing, I get.

The thing that shames me most about the time after Joe's death is that I can't remember where my children were or what they were doing. I am so grateful they were old enough to feed themselves! They were twenty-three and nineteen at the time and had jobs and places to live. But if they had still been dependent on me, I don't know if I could have pulled myself together or not. I prefer to think I could have.

I was not okay. Emily and Mark were not okay. We would not be okay for a very long time, and our *not okay-ness* would show itself in different ways; none of them shared and none of them good. I know now there was a need to share our grief, to acknowledge it, and talk about it, the three of us. But we didn't.

First Thessalonians 4:13 says that Christians are not supposed to grieve as the heathen (the unsaved) do, without hope. I knew where Joe was. He was with the Lord. Scripture taught that to be absent from the body is to be present with the Lord. I would see Joe again someday. I knew all that, but it wasn't helping. I wanted him with me right then!

We had prayed and prayed that he would be healed. People from all around the world had prayed that he would be healed. But God's answer to our prayers was to allow Joe to die. Joe had trusted God's will, and, as he had said, for him, whatever God's reasons were, they were good enough for him. But I was the one left alone, and I was mad at God.

I didn't stop believing in Him. I didn't turn my back on Him and stop talking to Him. But we were estranged; there was a definite coolness between us. Sometimes, I spoke to God rudely, angrily, disrespectfully.

On the surface, I behaved normally. I made decisions, carried out plans, paid the bills, and visited with my close friends. But being on the outs with my heavenly Father was a terrible time for me. I lost all my joy, peace, and enthusiasm for living. I felt like I was sleepwalking, and the world was colorless and grim, like a black-and-white war movie.

And yet the Lord continued to take care of me. When Joe died, we were about a million dollars in debt, mostly in medical bills. We had insurance, but copays built up, and it took a while for the insurance company to come through on such enormous hospital bills. But Cancer Treatment Centers of America wrote off every cent our insurance company did not pay. Joe's life insurance allowed me to pay off our mortgage.

I continued to work at the library for another year and taught at a private Christian school for a year, but what I was doing was going through the motions and waiting to feel better.

If the first year of grief was hard, the second year was even worse. The shock wore off, and I could feel all the pain of losing my husband / best friend / lover / co-parent / spiritual head / companion. I had read that the first and second years were the worst, but that things started getting better in the third year.

For the first six months of 2001, the third year, I didn't feel better, and I was still angry with the Lord, even while knowing how patient and tender He was being with me. But I did realize that I had to make some decisions about my future. I couldn't keep just wallowing around with no goals.

One day, some old friends who were associated with His Hill Bible School, in Comfort, Texas, invited me to come out for a visit. I went gladly, remembering prior years of Bible studies with these godly ladies. They asked questions about my life and what I planned to do with it.

I confessed I had been struggling with those very questions, since it had become obvious to me that God was not going to call me home to heaven just because Joe was there, despite my tears and tantrums. Finally, I finished my rant and said, "What am I going to do?"

The older, wise woman simply said, "You're going to attend Bible school."

What surprises me, even now, all these years later, was that I didn't even hesitate! I just said, "Okay, where shall I go?"

"Capernwray Hall Bible School in Northern England," she replied.

While I was being dumbfounded into silence, the other lady calmly said, "You know they have a waiting list," to which the first replied, "I'll write a letter."

And that was that. In a three-month period, I informed my family, resigned from my teaching job for the next year, sold my house, paid my tuition, bought a plane ticket, and landed in London in early September 2001.

I stayed with a friend, a British lady whom I knew from prior years when she had lived for a time in Boerne. On 9/11, we were at Salisbury Cathedral, getting a ticket for a tour when the attendant said something about, "You Yanks are really having a hard day." When I asked why, he told me about what had happened in New York City that morning.

I spent the next two days traveling north to Capernwray Hall, staying in youth hostels, and hearing people talking constantly about the attack on the World Trade Center and how the US had gotten what they deserved. That group was small but vocal, and it was very uncomfortable.

I finally got off the train in the little town of Carnforth, in Northern England, and was transported by a school staff person to a nineteenth-century castle, set in green rolling hills of grass and trees that made me think of the movie *Far and Away* every time I looked out a window. It was just lovely!

I had been informed when I was admitted that I would be, at fifty-six, the oldest student in the class, and the majority of the students had recently graduated from high schools all over the world. Capernwray Hall was the first of a system of Christian Bible schools that, by 2001, now operated in twenty-seven countries.

It was founded shortly after the end of World War II by British Major Ian Thomas, who was a devout Christian speaker and author. He had been asked by the new post-war German government to develop a program to educate German students about democracy. Major and Mrs. Joan Thomas decided to buy property where German youth could come to summer holiday programs and learn about democracy at the same time. The Thomases soon realized that the young people also needed to learn about Jesus Christ and His saving life.

Ian Thomas's main message, and the foundation of all his messages and books, was that, as Christians, we are not called to live the Christian life and, indeed, cannot! Only Christ can live the Christian life, and He saves us from our sin to live in us and to express His life through us, as we trust and respond to His love.

This word was water to my parched and weary soul, after nearly fifty years of churches who taught that we were saved to work our way to heaven and to earn our salvation.

The only thing I was afraid of in a school setting was that I might be rooming with a bunch of seventeen- and eighteen-year-olds who stayed awake and giggled all night. I was way too old for that! But God once again showed His mercy and lovingkindness to an undeserving old grouch by putting me in a room at the top of a tower with two lovely ladies in their forties who soon became my good friends.

We had a great time with all those teenagers, who were far from home and appreciated three quasi-moms who prayed for them, took them for coffee, listened to them, and made Christmas stockings stuffed with candy for them at Christmas.

Bible school was both a blessing and a burden for me. I loved what I was learning, but I was still grieving Joe and still at odds with the Lord. I cried every day at some point or another, and in a school with 180 kids, there weren't a lot of places to cry in peace!

I finally found a place at the top of the tower that had a spiral staircase that went all the way up past the third story to the roof, where the school flags were hung. There was a fantastic view from the roof, but for obvious reasons, in a school full of adolescents, the roof door was kept locked. But right outside that door was the top step of the spiral staircase where no one went but me. I would climb up there to pray and to cry.

One day, about two weeks after school started, I made an appointment with the principal and primary lecturer at the school. This fine gentleman had been teaching God's Word for all of his adult life and had been a pastor of a church for nearly fifty years. I had a burning question I wanted him to answer for me.

I walked into his office, introduced myself, and said, after no small talk at all, "Do you think there is ever a circumstance in life when God owes someone an apology?" The principal just sat and looked at me, saying nothing for a long time.

Finally, he said, "I've been a full-time pastor for nearly fifty years, and no one has ever asked me that question." Then he stood up, walked to a bookcase, pulled out a book, and handed it to me. It was a paperback copy of Leslie Weatherhead's *The Will of God*. "Read this and come back and talk to me."

I left without a word, read the book, and never had to go back. I took the book home with me and have shared the truths in it many times through the years.

The principal and I later became friends, and he has always been a source of God's wisdom and grace for me through the twenty years since Bible school.

Two months after school started, God intervened in my life to change my attitude completely. On November 1, 2001, I walked into the lecture hall where around two hundred people would shortly gather for the morning's first lecture. No one was there except for me, and it was very quiet. I noticed right away that every desk held a small green-covered book on its surface. I went to my desk, sat down, and opened the book. It was called *My Utmost for His Highest* and was written by Oswald Chambers. I immediately turned to the selection for November 1 and read it.

Here is the last section of the devotion that broke my heart and changed my mind:

> Why shouldn't we go through heart-breaks? Through these doorways God is opening up ways of fellowship with His Son. Most of us fall and collapse at the first grip of pain; we sit down on the threshold of God's purpose and die away of self-pity, and all so-called Christian sympathy will aid us to our death-bed. But God will not. He comes with the grip of the pierced hand of His Son, and says, "Enter into fellowship with Me; arise and shine." If through a broken heart God can bring His purposes to pass in the world, then thank Him for breaking your heart.

I knew three things immediately.

1. God was speaking to me through this passage.
2. He was asking me what He had been asking me repeatedly since my husband's death three years before. God was asking me to not only accept Joe's death as part of God's good and acceptable and perfect will (Romans 12:2); He was asking me to thank Him for breaking my heart.
3. He would not ask me again.

Numbers 1 and 2, I understood. Nothing was new there. But number 3 was different. That one had a consequence for the wrong answer. I had to know what that consequence would be.

I knew that God was faithful and would never leave me or desert me. But I also realized that our relationship would never be the same again if I refused His request. That would mean there was a limit to my devotion, to my willingness to obey, that I loved myself more than I loved Him, or that I didn't trust Him for His faithfulness to me. Like the man who looked back after putting his hand to the plow, it would make me unfit for service to the kingdom.

I was already standing on holy ground. There was a supernatural work going on in this room. Class was about to start. Was it possible that out of 180 students, I was the only one who showed up early this morning?

I stood up and said, "Lord, You know that I don't feel thankful for Joe's death. It would be a lie if I said I felt thankful. I don't feel thankful, but I can make a decision of my will to be thankful, and You will honor that decision and bring it to pass.

"So, Lord, because I trust You and I love You, I thank You for breaking my heart. I thank You for Joe's death, and I acknowledge that Your sovereign will is good and acceptable and perfect, no matter what it looks like or feels like to me."

At this point, I entered into what I can only call a vision. It seemed as if a huge gear shifted somewhere in heaven, the clouds rolled back, and bright and beautiful light began to shine through the windows. I suddenly realized that I had been in a dim, gloomy place for a long time, but now God's glory was shining in on me for the first time in almost three years.

It was exactly one month before the third anniversary of Joe's death. Those three years had been the darkest and most miserable of my entire life, not because of grief, but because of the estrangement—all on my side. Yes, I was grieving the loss of my beloved husband, but I was grieving as the heathen, the unsaved, do, as if there were nothing else to come, no eternal life, no heaven, no hope of ever seeing Joe again.

And, even worse, I was estranged from the Source of my life, my peace, my joy, my very being. In my pain and stubborn anger, I had turned away from the only One who could help me and save me from my self-inflicted misery. I blocked His light with my bitter anger.

God would have had every right to punish me by leaving me in the ash heap I had chosen for myself. But He didn't, not even for a second. He forgave my anger and my stubborn refusal to allow Him to comfort me. He took me into His arms and held me.

I was restored to full family privileges instantly, just as the prodigal son had been! There was no fatted calf, but there was full restoration, and what I learned in that empty classroom that day changed the course of my life.

Was I still grieving Joe? Yes, but not alone. I was in God's arms again, and that made all the difference.

Something else very important happened that day. I made a decision, the same decision that Joe had made and expressed shortly before his death: God's reasons for His actions—whatever they were, unknown to me, or known and not to my liking—would henceforth be good enough for me.

I would quarrel with my Maker no more. As Jesus had said to Paul on the road to Damascus, it was not good for me to kick against the pricks! It is disrespectful, painful, and useless! I was as unqualified in any manner to stand against the omnipotent God as a two-year-old to stamp his feet and scream with rage because his mother thought he needed a nap.

> "For my thoughts are not your thoughts, neither are your ways my ways," declares the LORD. "As the heavens are higher than the earth, so are my ways higher than your ways and my thoughts than your thoughts." Isaiah 55:8,9

It was really a relief to come to that decision because deep down inside, I knew it all the time.

The remainder of my time at Capernwray was much better than the first two months. I enjoyed the lectures and lecturers immensely, going deeper into the Christian faith that I had adhered to for more than forty years. I understood things I had never stopped to question and believed them even more than I had before.

I realized the greatness of the Savior and God I had been following for so long and found Him ever more wonderful than I had ever imagined. I made friends with students and staff members that I cherish and stay in contact with still, over twenty years later. If I had it to do all over again, I would do it in a minute, even at my current age of eighty. I didn't want it to end, but God had a plan for something else.

As June neared, the students began thinking about what they would do next. Some signed on with mission organizations for the next year, some planned to go home and marry their waiting sweethearts, and many of them were going on to university, college, or some other form of advanced education or career preparation.

I knew I wanted to go into some kind of service to God, and since I had training and experience as a clinical microbiologist, I was praying for an opportunity to go to Africa to work in a mission hospital. Little did I know that my daughter, son, parents, and sisters were begging God not to send me to any such place!

All I knew is that it was the last week of school, and students were celebrating where they were going next, and I knew nothing. One Sunday evening, at the evening worship service, the speaker talked about how foolish it was to try to dictate any course of action to God, when we should be surrendering to His will for whatever He wanted.

This was convicting to me, of course. Truth has a way of doing that! So after the service, I walked down the lane to the meadows in the quiet, spring darkness, and apologized to my Lord for, once again, trying to put my will before His. This will thing was taking more practice than I thought.

Anyway, it ended with my promising that I would say yes to the first opportunity that God sent my way, and I went back to my room with a lighter heart.

The very next day, my roommate and I were in our room when the loudspeaker informed us that Rita had a call from Bodenseehof, a sister Torchbearer Bible school in Germany. I said to my roommate, Liz, that it must be for her because she had been applying for a housekeeper's position at several of the European Bible schools.

Liz left, but soon came back, saying the call was for me, and it was the principal of Bodenseehof who said he would call back later. I had no clue why he would be calling me. I had met him once during the school year, when he came to lecture for a week. We happened to sit at the same table at lunch one day, with seven other students, and spoke very briefly.

But he did call back later that afternoon and said that he had been asking some of the female students at the end of school if there was anything that would have made the school year a better experience for them. They had said that “an older, English-speaking woman” to talk to would have helped.

As he had thought about it later, God had brought my name to mind, so he was calling to see if I would like to come and be that older, English-speaking woman and be a mentor to the female students.

It is amazing how many thoughts can fly through a person’s mind between sentences from someone else. I said to the Lord, “But I wanted to go to Africa!”

He said, “Just last night, didn’t you say you would say yes to the first opportunity I sent your way?”

“Yes, Lord, I did. Okay, I’ll go.” And to the principal, my new boss, “Sure, I’d love to do that!” I did ask one question, which I’m pretty sure came from the Lord because I had no idea I was going to say it: “Can I do some teaching?”

He said that I could, and asked me one question: “Do you have a warm coat?”

“Oh yes,” I said. (I didn’t have a warm coat, in his opinion. When he saw it, he laughed and took me to a store to buy one that he felt was adequate. I was glad when winter came. I had no idea how cold it got in Germany, but I knew I had never been that cold in my fifty-six years.)

So in early August, I packed up and flew off to Friedrichshafen, Germany, the home of Bodenseehof International Bible School. The principal picked me up at the airport and took me a few miles to the little village of Fischbach, right on Lake Bodensee, called Lake Constance in Switzerland.

I loved it immediately. It was a charming little town, set in beautiful countryside, with lots of wonderful places to walk. The school was in an apple orchard and had close access to the lake. When we walked in the front door, there was a long hall with a big bulletin board all along one wall. All the staff's photos were on this bulletin board, including mine. Under my picture were the words, "Mentor and Encourager."

It scared me half to death! I was a biology major, a clinical microbiologist, and a collector of insects, salamanders, and other crawling, slithering creatures. What was I doing here? From my distant perspective of hindsight, I know now what I was doing there. I was embarking on God's training course in dependency on Him, and Him alone.

He knew that when I thought I knew what I was doing, I invariably got into trouble. Two years with teens separated from their parents by a very wide ocean were wildly beyond my ken. My prayer life improved rapidly.

On the first day of the fall term, the students arrived, about eighty of them, seventeen to eighteen years old, with varying amounts of maturity among them. Some were already homesick, some were scared of being in a strange place with strange other people, and some thought they were *all that* with a bow attached.

I was in my *office*, also my room, when a young lady knocked on my door, saying that the principal had sent her to see me. We sat down, and I asked her how I might help her. She looked straight into my eyes and said, "I've been hurting myself." I asked her how she was hurting herself, and she pulled up her sleeve and said, "I've been cutting myself." Her arm was covered with scabbed-over cuts from her inner elbow to her wrist.

My mind flew to God, and I said, "You've got to do this! I don't know what to say! Please!"

My mouth opened, and I said, "Did you bring anything with you to hurt yourself with here at school?" She said that she had brought her knives with her, and I asked her to tell me why she hurt herself.

She told me a story of abuse and betrayal by those she should have been able to trust, not her family, but other adults responsible for her. When she reported the abuse, she was not believed.

God kept giving me things to say to this heartbroken young lady. The voice was mine, but the words were His. We prayed together. I asked her if she would let me keep her knives for her until school was over, and she said she would.

She went and got them, and when she showed them to me, I was chilled all over. I had never seen any knives like them. They had hooks on the blades to make even more painful wounds. They looked demonic to me. She left them with me.

I kept an eye on her during the term, and she seemed to be enjoying her classmates and had a close relationship with the other girls in her room. We spoke occasionally, and I felt at peace about her.

On the last day of school, she came to my room and asked me if she could have her knives. I asked her what she was going to do with them, and she said she and her roommates were going to go to the lake, and she was going to throw them in. I asked if I could go along, and she said I could.

It was a happy occasion. Her roommates were very supportive and encouraging, and I could tell that God had healed and freed her of the damage she had suffered.

That was my baptism of fire into mentoring and encouraging, and I knew God would be there for me, no matter what happened or what I would face, if I would depend upon Him and not upon my own abilities.

All in all, my experiences at Bodenseehof were very positive. The staff were all great people, all of them younger than me, and I was able to help them with various things from time to time. Several of them are very good friends still today.

But I was not there to have a good time, and it was not all sunshine every day. Bodenseehof was the place and the time of my life when I learned I was not my own. You would have thought by the age of fifty-six, I would have found that out already.

I had known God for a long time and had lots of experiences with Him that were meaningful, eventful, and impactful. Some of them were frightening, life-threatening, and painful, but apparently, I still had some things to learn, if I was willing to learn them, and I was. God is so very good at working His plan out in our lives in the right order so that the circumstances all fit together and make sense.

I was at Bodenseehof to serve the Lord by serving the students. I just thought I would do this on a schedule. I was a list and a schedule maker. I kept a calendar on which I wrote appointments and assignments and crossed them out as I accomplished them. I got up early and wanted to be in bed by 10:00 p.m.

The early part usually worked because students are not notoriously early risers, and I was able to write lectures, read my Bible, study, and take my usual solitary walks in the mornings. Occasionally, being out and about early meant I saw what the students had been up to before any other staff members were up to see it.

One morning, the boys had swapped all the main floor furniture, which included the dining room and lecture hall, for the basement furniture, which was the student lounge areas, prayer room, and activity areas. This meant that breakfast would be severely delayed, and the cooking staff would be severely annoyed.

I had the unhappy duty of waking the dean of students to inform him of the situation, which was bound to complicate his morning to a large degree. In this case, the punishment fit the crime in that breakfast was not served until the mess was completely resolved, and the main miscreants caught it in the neck from all sides by hungry, grumpy students and staff. It was really rather funny, but it never happened again!

Being available to the students meant that my schedule meant nothing. I rarely got to bed by ten because students would need someone to talk to when they were finished with their activities and that could be later than my (hopeful) bedtime. I didn't mind, but I did get tired.

Once in a while, I would find myself lying on my bed while a young couple hashed out their problems while I listened and prayed. All this to say, I quickly learned that the world did not operate on my schedule, did not care if I was tired, rarely made appointments, and often did not keep the ones they made.

And amazingly enough, this was the way it was supposed to be. My life and my time were not my own. It was God's schedule, and I was God's bondservant, one who had been set free from slavery and chose to remain a servant even though they were free.

The Lord had set me free from the bondage of sin and was now setting me free from self so that I might willingly choose to be His servant. It was sometimes a painful process. I remember saying to the Lord, "Father, I think I'm going to get hurt here."

He answered, "Yes, you are, but it won't last for long, and it is necessary for My purposes to be accomplished." And they were.

After two years, God said that my time at Bodenseehof was reaching an end, so in early April, I packed up my things, except for two large boxes of books, which I shipped home. I flew to Manchester, England, and stayed for about a month at Capernwray.

I might have stayed longer, but one morning, I received a phone call from my daughter, telling me that my father was seriously ill, and I needed to come home. I immediately made a reservation to fly home, said my goodbyes to my staff friends at Capernwray Hall, got a ride to the Manchester airport, and was in Boerne, Texas, by the end of the day.

Six-hour time difference allows for time *miracles*!

I returned to the duplex where I had been living before my European adventures had begun and where my roommate, a friend of many years, had been living in my absence. I was greeted by one of the big boxes of books, but the other one didn't show up for two months and looked like it had made a detour to India on its trip to Texas. I was very glad to see it!

In the meantime, much had happened. I had taken over the clinic visits at Lackland Air Force Base with my dad, where he had many tests, been *diagnosed* with cancer, and finally had surgery, which revealed a completely blocked bile duct but no cancer. After the blockage was cleared, Daddy recovered and happily went back to his garden.

But something else happened during that time of clinic and hospital visits that was to change the lives of our entire family. One day, during the weeks of lab tests and scans that my dad underwent, Mom and I were sitting in a waiting room while Dad was having another test. Suddenly, she looked up at me and said, "Now tell me why we are here?"

It is amazing how fast the human brain can function sometimes. The word that appeared in my mind in an instant was *Alzheimer's*. It must have been a message from God because I knew it was right, even though, at that time, Mom had exhibited no other symptoms of dementia. Or so I thought. I later learned that my daughter and niece, who had helped Mom with Thanksgiving dinner the preceding year, had noticed some differences in Mom's speech and behavior but had attributed it to fatigue.

But shortly after Mom's question at the clinic, it became apparent that something was amiss. Mom began forgetting how to do things she had done for years, like operate the microwave. One day, while trying to heat her lukewarm coffee, she had set the timer for three hours and burned the microwave up. And when I told Emily, my daughter, about it, she said that Mom had done it once before! My dad had called Emily, told her to get rid of the ruined microwave, and gave her money to go and get a new one. And that was his reaction to the second fried appliance too. "Get rid of it, and go buy a new one," he said.

I did that, of course, but I also made an appointment for Mom with my family doctor in Boerne. He examined Mom, had her do the standard *clock test*, and gave her three words to remember for ten minutes. Mom failed both tests. The doctor and I talked about it, and he prescribed Aricept for her, to "slow the process of the disease," and we went home.

I told my dad what was happening and told him I was moving in with them to take care of Mom and him, since he couldn't cook, and Mom shouldn't! It was what needed to happen, and I was the logical choice of caregiver, since

I was widowed and lived in Boerne, while my two younger sisters still had husbands to care for and lived in other cities in Texas.

Knowing it was the logical choice, the right thing to do, didn't make me rejoice to do it. I was apprehensive, not about caring for my mother, but I knew I would have trouble living with my retired chief master sergeant father, whom my sisters and I fondly called *the benevolent tyrant*. Daddy loved his three girls, was very proud of our accomplishments, and always wanted the best for us. The problem was that he always knew what the best was for us.

We three girls responded to this autocratic benevolence in different ways. The youngest sister never did anything wrong, and she and her husband were in church work, full-time ministry, so Dad pretty much left them to God. The middle sister did exactly as she wanted to at all times and ignored Dad's instructions and advice. I, as the oldest, avoided conflict as much as possible but occasionally went toe to toe with Dad and never settled anything!

I moved in with Mom and Dad and prayed that God would not only let me survive but thrive. I lived with them for eight years, from 2004 until 2012. My mother passed away in September of 2011, and my father in January of 2012. Dad gave up living when my mother died, but his body held on a few months longer.

He fell frequently as he approached ninety-two, and one night after Mom was gone, he fell in his bedroom. I heard him calling and went to help, but it took almost an hour for Dad to get back onto his bed, with me pushing and pulling, him crawling, because I wasn't strong enough to get him back on his feet. We eventually got him up on his bed, with both of us totally exhausted and breathless.

After a few minutes, Dad said, "Why doesn't God just take me home?"

My filters were apparently worn-out too because I answered, "Well, Daddy, maybe God just wants to be in charge a while longer." That was the last time I ever heard my father laugh.

He fell again in January, breaking his hip. The Boerne ER sent him off to the hospital in San Antonio by ambulance, with no other symptoms besides the broken hip. By the time Dad arrived at the hospital, his heart was in A-fib, and his kidneys were failing. He was admitted to the medical ICU in a lot of pain, but he couldn't have pain meds because the surgeon was planning to fix his hip as soon as the A-fib and kidney issues were resolved.

I was there with him by myself, and Dad was unconscious but moaning and moving around like he was uncomfortable. I said to the ICU nurse, who was a very kind young man, "Can't you give him something for the pain?"

He said, "Is that what you want for your dad?"

I said, "Of course!"

He looked at me and said, "Then what are you doing here?"

It was like he had shaken me awake. I thought, *What am I doing here? Is this what Dad would want?* I knew he had previously signed a DNR. I said to the nurse, "What can I do?" In a very short time, the unit director had contacted Hospice for us, they had gone to my dad's home and set up a hospital bed, and we had transported my still unconscious but now pain-free father to his home, where a hospice nurse waited to evaluate him and keep him medicated against pain.

I had called my sisters, and they had agreed with my decision and would come the next day. This was a Friday evening, and the hospice nurse said she didn't think my dad would live much longer. I was not comfortable giving Daddy narcotics, so the nurse stayed with him for two more days, until he peacefully passed away in the early hours of Monday morning.

There was really no reason for our father to die when he did. He was healthy until he broke his hip and had no other conditions that would have ended his life. Knowing Daddy as we did, my sisters and I figured that he had decided to die, so he did. It was just like him to do that. Mom was gone; his mission was complete; it was time to go.

After all the legal things associated with our father's will and settling the estate were done, my two sisters and I took on the monumental task of clearing out the house our parents had lived in for nearly forty years. Both of Mom's and Dad's mothers and one great-aunt had died during those years, so our parents had the remnants of three households in their own home. It was almost overwhelming, but two husbands and several daughters pitched in to help, and eventually, it was done. The house was empty. We were just about to put it on the market and had agreed on a real estate agent when a coworker of my daughter, Emily, asked to look at the house and made an immediate good offer on it. We were done!

I was done too, out of a job completely. And still in a good frame of mind and not too crazy yet. The Lord had done just the right thing to prepare me for eight years with my sweet but forgetful mother and my autocratic but mentally sharp father. In other words, in a situation where I had very little control over anything but my own attitude. I was adequately prepared by the time I had spent at Bodenseehof as an encourager and mentor to a group of teenagers with needs that went on day and night. I could never guarantee I could keep to a schedule or keep an appointment. My life was mostly not my own.

Does that sound familiar? First Corinthians 6:19 says,

> Do you not know that your body is the temple of the Holy Spirit, Who lives within you, Whom you have received as a gift from God? You are not your own.

I had read that verse many times before, but it was at Bodenseehof that I truly experienced the truth of that scripture. And it was in my parents' home that I experienced God's will for my life to an even greater degree—to be His servant in every way. I truly was not my own. I am not my own now. If we belong to Christ, we are never our own. We can harbor no resentment. We can hold nothing back. We can question no request.

> We are bought with a price—purchased with a preciousness, (the very blood of Jesus) and paid for, made His own. So then, honor God and bring glory to Him in your body. (1 Corinthians 6:20)

When I surrendered the ownership of my body to God, I found a great side effect to that transfer of authority. God takes total responsibility for the person who cedes ownership to Him. I am able to be singularly worry-free in the ins and outs of my life. God is in charge, and He takes very good care of me. He protects me and provides for me. He listens to me when I need to talk and is my wisdom. The more I depend upon Him, the more dependable He proves to be. The Scripture says that God is my spouse and my keeper, and that's a big job, since I have neither one of those positions filled in my single life. But God is more than adequate at taking care of His children and does a very good job of meeting all our needs from His riches in glory (Philippians 4:19).

What did God have for me to do next in my life? For a while, I just rested because I was pretty much exhausted, physically, mentally, and emotionally.

Dear friends from England, Germany, and Austria came to visit at different times, and I loved introducing them to Texas. My German friend was a lady several years younger than me, whom I had gotten to know at Bodenseehof, where her husband was the director of the Bible school. The very day she got off the plane and we were driving home, I spotted a cottonmouth water moccasin sunning on a log near a stream in a wooded area we were passing through. I took the opportunity to point the snake out to my friend and to also warn her about rattlesnakes and coral snakes, both of which live in the area of my home.

Another day, we were taking a walk, and I pointed out the Texas prickly poppy, a lovely flower with sharp, thorny prickles on its stem. Walking into a patch of them can be a very painful experience. After that came fire ants, black widow spiders, brown recluse spiders, red wasps, poison ivy, and poison oak. My friend was very quiet for a while and then said, "Does everything in Texas bite or sting or stick you?" She was also horrified by the amount of food served in restaurants. I literally watched her face turn pale when a waiter put down a plate of pancakes in front of her and had to assure her that no one would be offended if she didn't eat it all.

I was able to make several visits to England and Germany to visit the two Bible schools where I had attended or worked and one great trip to help with wedding preparations and attend the wedding of my wonderful friend and flatmate at

Bodenseehof. It was wonderful to see all my dear friends, who were so influential in my spiritual growth, and to spend time with them again.

In 2017, I moved from Boerne to Mason, Texas, where my son and his family lived. I found an apartment very near the school where my granddaughter and grandson attended and happily became the after-school snack-making, homework-helping, hug-giving grandmother—or *Grammy*, as the kids called me.

I loved Mason, a very small but busy town out in the red sand country, where there were lots of mesquite trees, rattlesnakes, and cattle. I drove one of the few sedans in town, as pickup trucks were the predominant mode of transportation. Not that there were a whole lot of vehicles in town. If there were more than two at a stop sign, it was a traffic jam! The people were friendly, there were lots of small churches, it was safe for walking, and I quickly felt at home there.

I attended a church that had bought the old high school building and met some very loving people who became good friends. I lived in Mason for two years and enjoyed it thoroughly, but I missed my friends of fifty years' duration back in Boerne. When the kids had advanced to middle school and were very busy and no longer in need of an after-school babysitter, I moved back to a smaller town than Mason called Comfort, which was only fifteen miles from Boerne.

This came about as a piece of divine engineering when an old friend asked if Emily and I would like to rent the house on the same property where she lived, near another Bible school and summer camp that our family had strong ties to, called His Hill. So in August of 2019, which is the absolute worst time in Texas to move anything, much less two households, because it is so awfully hot and humid, Emily and I moved to the country, where the deer and the antelope play.

Well, not antelope, but lots of deer, plus wild pigs, squirrels, rabbits, snakes, coyotes, skunks, porcupines, armadillos, foxes, the occasional mountain lion, various rodents, and many species of birds, including hummingbirds that quickly found us and became demanding, albeit charming, permanent frequenters of our front porch. And if the feeders were not filled on time, one hummer would come looking for me. I would look up from the kitchen sink or the backyard garden hose to find a cranky bird hovering in front of me.

Twice, we have had snakes in hot pursuit of rodents on our porch. They were nonvenomous, so we said, "Thank you," and got out of their way.

The best thing about our home, which is beautiful in itself, is its setting. There is a canyon that runs parallel to our yard. The rim is about thirty feet from the front porch and front door of the house, and the canyon is filled with trees that are just gorgeous in the fall. The sun sets behind the hills on the other side of the canyon, so the porch is perfectly situated for sunset watching. And in the morning, I walk out the back door onto a deck and watch the sun come up.

The amazing and wonderful thing about this house is that it was built for a retreat center, and I first came to it forty years ago. I fell in love with the house and its beautiful setting and remember asking the Lord to let me live there someday. Now forty years later, I do! I thank Him every time I walk outside for the opportunity to spend my declining years, as some have called them, in such a lovely environment. It is a gift…His gift.

I hope to live here for the rest of my life, and I have told my daughter that I want to leave here feet first. She said that was okay with her, but I had to stay alive until I was ninety-two, which was my father's age when he died. I'm fine with that, but as I pointed out to Emily, since I don't have access to God's book where the days of my life were recorded even before my creation (Psalm 139:16), I can't make any promises! Neither do I have any idea of God's future earthly plans for me. But, as I have said, I have lived in the goodness of God for my whole life, and I trust that goodness will continue for all eternity. So whatever He has for me, I will be content. If He allows me to stay where I am now, I will be ecstatically content!

This is pretty much where I am, up to this part of my autobiography, which, as I said in the beginning, I have written to relate God's gracious dealings in my life, despite my sometimes lack of cooperation and appreciation. God is good, period. And even though there were periods in my life when my attitude was poor and my obedience worse, He has been faithful to me and has worked to bring me back to the paths of blessedness, despite myself.

So here I am, a happy old lady, eighty years old, in what my health practitioners call *fragile health*, due to the age thing plus fifteen years, so far, of type 1 diabetes, which they tell me makes my potential life span shorter. Some days, I feel like agreeing with them, and some days, I feel good, and I don't agree. But that is neither here nor there to me. I will walk, crawl, or lie down in the goodness of God for all the days of my life, and I will die on the day ordained for my death and written in His book for me—not a day sooner or later. And whatever the circumstance of my death may be, it won't be the cause of my death. The cause will be that the One who made me has called me home.

So the end of this part of the book has come. Now on to the last part: What are my beliefs, and the practices that have come out of those beliefs that have brought me to my life of whatever you want to call it, be it happiness, joy, contentment, or all three, despite the requisite difficulties of life on a fallen planet, plus a few more brought on by my own foolishness and sin? Or to put it much more simply: Why am I such a happy old lady?

I did not plan for this book to be an autobiography, and when I discovered that was what it was becoming, I stopped writing it for almost a year. I did not think that the story of my life would be interesting or instructive to anyone except my family members who love me and are stuck with me. Finally, a conversation with a wise, longtime friend convinced me that my attitude on this subject was incorrect, and if that was what appeared when I had prayed for guidance, then I should keep writing.

I prayed and thought some more, kept writing, and a pattern appeared. My story was not just my story. It was the story of God's dealings in my life that led me to become the person He created me to be. I had always thought that circumstances were just things that happened to happen! Monumental shortsightedness for an old lady who had lived through some pretty meaningful things in her eighty years and had been a Christian through nearly seventy of those years.

It's not that I didn't know the relevant Scriptures about the sovereignty of God, the will of God, or His plans for His children's lives. I just had a huge blind spot about what they meant to my life. Satan is very good at blinding our *eyes*, perceptions, and thoughts, especially when self-will is involved. The events (circumstances) that I include in my life story illustrate how God got my attention and, while He had it, taught me what I needed to know about who I was, Who He was, and just what that obvious huge difference meant in having an actual relationship with my Creator, Savior, and Lord.

One day not too long ago (I think, at least; in some subjects, I am a slow learner), I was complaining about something that was going on in my life that I was not happy about. No one was present in the room except for me and the Lord, so I must have been complaining to Him. He is remarkably patient and merciful! Anyway, I went on and on, until I finally paused for breath, and I heard in my mind God say very clearly, "Circumstances are Mine. Responses are yours."

God chooses what happens in this world. He chooses what happens in my life and in the lives of every single person in the world. That's what sovereignty is: complete control. God has complete control over the entire world and all that is in it, except for the will of human beings. God has given free will to us, His creations made in His image.

What does this mean in terms of circumstances that are under the control of God and that come into our lives whether we want them to or not? It means just what He said: "Circumstances are Mine. Responses are yours." I am given free will to choose my response to what God is allowing in my life—my circumstances. And what is really involved in any situation is trust. Do I trust Him—His love, His wisdom, and His power—enough to accept whatever the circumstances might be as God's good for my life? The answer to that question is the answer to all of life's thorny questions. Do we trust Him enough to obey Him?

I learned recently that the circumstances that God allows in our lives before we are saved are to lead us to a saving knowledge of Jesus Christ. That makes sense to me. But then, why do things keep happening after we are saved that are unpleasant, uncomfortable, and even painful and dangerous?

Shortly thereafter, I read the answer to that question, and once again, it made sense. (It doesn't need to make sense; the fact that God is behind it is more than enough. I just happen to like things to make sense to my finite mind.) Just as circumstances before salvation have a very definite purpose in our lives, circumstances after salvation also have a function that is every bit as important. God uses our post-salvation circumstances to change our character, reactions, behaviors, and attitudes to be the same as those of Jesus Christ.

Every single thing that crosses our will, makes us cranky, discontented, unhappy, frightens us, or evokes a self-centered response, brings on a temper tantrum, or immature behavior, happens so that we will have the opportunity to learn to allow the Lord to express His perfect character within us. As we are convicted, confess, and repent, we are given the opportunity to change and grow into the likeness of our Savior and Lord.

The eventual outcome for future circumstances is that we will learn to trust God with whatever is happening and walk in the character and attitudes of the Lord. There will be no temper tantrums in heaven! So the circumstances are provided by God with the purpose being that my responses are becoming sanctified, which means being made holy—just like Jesus. No way around it!

Our best, really only, viable option is to do what Elisabeth Elliot said over and over again throughout her life, even when her young husband was killed by tribesmen in the Amazon: "Trust and obey." Job said it too, in different words, when his whole world lay in pieces around him:

> Yield now and be at peace with Him. (Job 22:21)

To trust and obey is the highest calling for every Christian, the calling that makes everything else possible. We can do no great things for God until we say these words to Him: "Lord, I will trust You in all things, and because I trust You, I can and will obey You."

# *Believing and Receiving the Abundant Life of Jesus Or How to Be a Happy Old Lady*

When I was at Bodenseehof, a wonderful speaker named Ray Andrews came to lecture and minister to the students and the staff. Dr. Ray Andrews is the executive director of NEWLife Training and Counselling and ministers extensively around the world, helping churches and believers live in the freedom Jesus came to die that we might have—abundant life on this earth, and life with Him forever in eternity. His *Abiding Life—Identity Seminar* builds on what the Christian has—the Lord Jesus living *in* the believer, resident, and abiding there by personal invitation. There is nothing that the nearness of the Lord will not cure.

In one lecture, Dr. Andrews made a statement that hit me right between the eyes. He said—and I paraphrase now—that all Christians were on their way to heaven, but that many of them were living in hell while on earth. He went on to explain that the reason for this was that they were not believing the truths of God's Word and not receiving God's promises and blessings. Even though they had believed the Bible concerning redemption by the blood of Jesus Christ and had received Him into their hearts, they had quit there.

They didn't believe John 10:10 about abundant life in Him right here on earth.

Hearing this explained a lot to me. I had noticed that there was a lot of angst, drama, and tears going on in our student body, and as I talked to these unhappy kids, which was my job, that while they were saved, they were definitely not living in the good of the gospel.

That was where I was called to talk to Christians about believing and receiving not only the truth of salvation by grace alone but also about believing and receiving what some have called the rest of the gospel. I started with myself. I discovered that there were lies I was still believing, even after being a Christian for many years. I believed I was God's child but not necessarily everything that God said about me as His child.

I did not feel adequate or holy and certainly not worthy of my salvation or any of God's other gifts. I was afraid of many things and lacked the courage to step out and do certain things. I felt like God loved me as one of His millions of redeemed souls, but not especially me, as a person. I was not a particularly peaceful, joyful believer. In other words, I wasn't living the abundant life Jesus died and rose again to give me.

But I wanted to be!

And I told God so. I told Him my longings to believe and receive every single thing He had for me and asked Him to accomplish this great work in me. I think maybe I heard Him say, "And about time too!" And in His grace and mercy and love, my Abba has opened my mind and heart to understand and receive what He means for all His children to have—a close, special, intimate fellowship and companionship with Him.

In C. S. Lewis's last book of *The Chronicles of Narnia*, *The Last Battle*, the old world of Narnia has come to an end. All of those who love Aslan, who is the Christ figure in the books, have come into Aslan's country, which we would call heaven. Aslan comes to meet them, and after a little while with the main characters, He says to them, "Children, you don't look as happy as I want you to be." The children hem and haw and shuffle their feet, and finally, one of them admits that they are afraid they won't be allowed to stay. They fear they will have to return to Earth. In other words, all of this was just too good to be true.

I think sometimes we think that way. Salvation, heaven, *and* earthly blessings too? Surely, we are not worthy of God's love, of Jesus's sacrificial death on the Cross, and of all the love, mercy, grace, friendship, intimacy, and blessings too! Well, let me help you with this *not-worthy* issue, as Malcolm Smith helped me—and maybe some of you. He said,

> Worthy? Of course, you're not worthy! None of us are, in ourselves. God has made us worthy—we are worthy in His sight because of our redemption in Jesus.

It is all based on our redemption in Jesus. God's love for us is not based on our behavior or our attitude. It is based on our position in Christ, not our condition. This is such good news!

The keys to the kingdom, to abundant life in Christ, are to believe and receive. Believe what God says, receive what God gives—all on the basis of redemption. Because we are His through the redemption of His blood, and He loves us and wants to have a close and personal relationship with us, is the beginning point to the abundant life Jesus is referring to in John 10:10, which says in the Amplified Bible,

> The thief comes only in order that he may steal and may kill and may destroy. I came that they may have and enjoy life, and have it in abundance, to the full, till it overflows.

Our Savior and Lord, Jesus Christ the Messiah, died not only to atone for our sins so that we might live with Him forever, but He rose again so that we might have abundant life in Him and through Him right here on earth. He wants us to have and enjoy our earthly lives to the full and overflowing.

Matthew 4:25 says about Jesus, "And great crowds joined and accompanied Him about…" In Matthew 5:1–11, we find what is called the Sermon on the Mount, given by Jesus to this crowd of people who flocked to hear Him. This passage is also called *The Beatitudes*. The definition of *beatitude* in the *Merriam-Webster Dictionary* is "a state of utmost bliss." The synonyms of *beatitude* are *blessedness, bliss, blissfulness, felicity, gladness, happiness, joy*, and, of all things, *warm fuzzies*! It boggles the mind!

Matthew 5:3, in the Amplified Bible, says this:

> Blessed—happy, to be envied, and spiritually prosperous (that is, with life-joy and satisfaction in God's favor and salvation, regardless of their outward conditions)—are the poor in spirit (the humble, rating themselves insignificant), for theirs is the kingdom of heaven!

The next ten verses continue in the same vein, using similar adjectives to describe the abundant life that Jesus died and rose again to give His children—those who received Him as Savior and Lord. Each verse also tells the kind of person that will receive these blessings, and it was these verses that signaled to the listening crowds and to the listening world for the last two thousand years, give or take a few years, who Jesus really was and what kind of people would accept Him and His kingdom: the humble, those who mourn, the meek, those who hunger and thirst for righteousness, the merciful, the pure in heart, the peacemakers, and the persecuted. Wealth, power, and influence were not mentioned.

Is it any wonder that Jesus was put to death less than three years later, by an unholy and very unlikely alliance of the Roman Empire and the ruling religious leaders of Israel? Jesus was a dangerous man. He was also the Son of God and the coming King, co-Creator and Ruler of the universe. And that One is the very One who loves you and me, died for us, and wants to give us Himself as our source of abundant (blessed, happy, to be envied, and spiritually prosperous, with life-joy and satisfaction in God's favor and salvation) life.

And believing and receiving (adopting, reveling in, basking in) that good news is definitely on the "Rita, the Happy Old Lady" list. But it is not at the top of the list because the first thing on the Happy Old Lady list is the name given in the very first verse of the Bible:

God is the Creator of the universe.

> In the beginning, God created the heavens and the earth. (Genesis 1:1)

The Hebrew word for *God* used here is *Elohim* and is translated plurally, as "In the beginning Gods created the heavens and the earth." God the Father, God the Son, and God the Holy Spirit—the blessed Trinity—created the heavens and the earth. One in essence, in character, yet three persons united as One, *Elohim* is God as Creator. My whole life is based on the truth that God exists, has always existed, and created the entire universe.

God is the Sovereign ruler of the universe.

> Know ye that the LORD Himself is God. It is He that has made us, and not we ourselves; We are His people and the sheep of His pasture. (Psalm 100:3)

> Our God is in the heavens; He does all that He pleases. (Psalm 115:3)

> Many are the plans in the mind of a man, but it is the purposes of the LORD that will stand. (Proverbs 19:21)

> Remember the former things of old; for I am God, and there is no other; I am God, and there is none like Me, declaring the end from the beginning and from ancient times things not yet done, saying, "My counsel shall stand, and I will accomplish all My purpose." (Isaiah 46:9–10)

> All the inhabitants of the earth are accounted as nothing, and He does according to His will among the host of heaven and among the inhabitants of the earth; and none can stay His hand or say to Him, "What have You done?" (Daniel 4:35)

Those verses proclaim that God is in control of everything, seen and unseen. As His child, it is very reassuring to know that my Father is the ruler of all the universe and everything in it. Nothing and no one is higher, stronger, or more powerful than God.

> What shall we then say to these things? If God be for us, who can be against us? Romans 8:31

My entire security is based on the truth that God is in control of the universe and that He is all-powerful, all-wise, and all-loving.

God is love.

> "Can anything ever separate us from Christ's love:" Does it mean He no longer loves us if we have trouble or calamity, or are persecuted, or hungry, or destitute, or in danger, or threatened with death?
>
> (As the Scriptures say, "For Your sake we are killed every day; we are being slaughtered like sheep.) No, despite all

> these things, overwhelming victory is ours through Christ Who loved us.
>
> And I am convinced that nothing can ever separate us from God's love. Neither death nor life, neither angels or demons, neither our fears for today nor our worries about tomorrow—not even the powers of hell can separate us from God's love.
>
> No power in the sky above or in the earth below—indeed nothing in all creation will ever be able to separate us from the love of God that is revealed in Christ Jesus our Lord. (Romans 8:35–39)

> God is love, and the one who abides in love abides in God, and God abides in Him. (1 John 4:16c)

And, finally, that crowning verse about the love of God for His creatures made in His own image and graced by His love:

> For God so loved the world that He gave His only begotten Son, that whosoever believes in Him should not perish, but have everlasting life. (John 3:16)

The entire happiness of my life is based on the conviction of God's love for me.

God is light.

> This is the message we have heard from Him and announce to you, that God is Light, and in Him is no darkness at all. If we say that we have fellowship with Him and yet walk in the darkness, we lie and do not practice the truth; but if we walk in the Light as He Himself is in the Light, we have fellowship with one another, and the blood of Jesus His Son cleanses us from all sin. (1 John 1:5–7)

God is light, and in Him is no darkness at all. No darkness at all—no falsehoods, no hedging, no half-truths, no deceit, no dissembling, no ulterior motives. We never have to wonder about what God is really thinking, what is really behind His Words. He is as He says He is. What He says, He will do. There is no shadow of turning with God. What we see is what He is. No darkness at all. God is transparent.

I can trust Him with my life and my happiness because He is completely trustworthy.

God is good.

> Oh, taste and see that the Lord is good! Blessed is the man who takes refuge in Him. (Psalm 34:8)

> The Lord is good to all, and His mercy is over all that He had made. (Psalm 145:9)

> Every good gift and every perfect gift is from above, coming down from the Father of lights, with whom there is no variation or shadow due to change. (James 1:17)

> For the Lord God is a sun and a shield; the Lord bestows favor and honor. No good thing does He withhold from those who walk uprightly. (Psalm 84:11)

> Do not be conformed to this world, but be transformed by the renewal of your mind, that by testing you may discern what is the will of God, what is good and acceptable and perfect. (Romans 12:2)

God is good. Everything about Him is good. His works are good, His actions are good, His character is good, His motives are good, and His plans for our lives are good. One caveat: God's definitions are not always the same as ours, and *good* has one of those definitions. *Good*, to God, means being able to fulfill His purposes, not just to make one feel good.

So in order to understand God's definition of *good*, we have to read Romans 8:28–30:

> And we know that God causes all things to work together for good to those who love God and are called according to His purpose.
>
> For whom He foreknew, He also predestined to become conformed to

> the image of His Son, that He might be the first-born among many brethren and whom He predestined, these He also called, and whom He called, these He also justified; and whom He justified, these He also glorified.

So we see that God does cause all things to work together for good to those who love God, not for a *good* that just makes us feel good but a *good* with the purpose of conforming us to the image of His Son. This is a passage with a great deal of *gravitas* because it is the meaning of sanctification, which is the final step of the salvation process. Christians are being sanctified—made holy—every day of their lives, so that, when we die, we will enter heaven without spot or blemish.

All of my earthly life, and even before I was born, I have lived in the goodness of the God who has known me from the beginning of the world.

I obviously have a lot of good biblical reasons for feeling blessed, happy, and content. The Bible is full of them, and I've barely scratched the surface of what I have included here. But as we all know, just reading and knowing the Scriptures does not guarantee feeling good about the condition of one's mind, soul, or body. What we believe can be twisted, diluted, doubted, or just flat lost.

We see it often in the Christian community. Strong, active believers just drift away and don't come back. What happens? Proverbs 4:23 gives us a clue:

> Above all else, guard your heart, for everything you do flows from it.

Another translation flat out says, "Guard your thoughts; they run your life!" I like that translation because it is alarming, and it should be!

We have an enemy—the devil, that old liar—who is out to rip us away from God who loves us. And it is because God loves us that Satan is so determined to pull us away from God and damage our relationship with Him. Satan does not care anything about us at all. C. S. Lewis says the enemy only sees us as food—something to be destroyed and devoured. And there are lots of us, so no big deal. But the big deal comes from the truth that God loves us. God knows we are dust, but He loves His little dust people. Satan knows that too and sees in that love an opportunity to hurt the One he hates the most, God.

Now despite what we read or see in movies or on TV, Satan and his demons cannot actually kill humans or even hurt us physically. Humans do not come into danger from the enemy until and unless we die apart from our Savior's redeeming love. No, Satan cannot hurt us, but he can make us hurt ourselves. And he has no weapons against us except his great intelligence, his careful observation of us throughout our lives, and the lies he tells us.

And that is why we must guard our thoughts at all costs. Satan knows all our weak spots, our insecurities, our sins, our past mistakes, and he will whisper your worst fears into your ear. He will recite your sins to you and then say, "God could never love a ______________ like you." And the word you are most terrified for God to hear will be in that blank.

You better know the truth that God will never leave you or desert you, and the truth that nothing can ever separate you from the love of God. You better remember the verse that says,

> If we confess our sins, He is faithful and righteous to forgive us our sins and to cleanse us from all unrighteousness. (1 John 1:9)

Guard your thoughts, and remember that God loves you and that there is no condemnation for those who are in Christ Jesus.

A last thought about our thoughts:

> Most of your unhappiness in life is due to the fact that you are listening to yourself instead of talking to yourself. (Martyn Lloyd-Jones)

This is true because most of the time, when we are listening to ourselves, it is actually the enemy speaking lies to us, or we're making excuses or telling lies to ourselves. We can, however, speak truth to ourselves if we have put truth into our minds. Our minds are like computers: What is downloaded is what is going to appear on the screen! So if we are going to give ourselves a good talking-to, we need to have something in our minds worth listening to. Scripture is always truth and always reflects the mind of the Author, so it will never fail us, lie to us, or lead us in the wrong direction.

I've been thinking a lot about being a happy old lady, or not, and I have made a few observations about the question. Happiness is generally predicated on the conditions or situations, difficulties, emotions involved, bodily conditions, state of loved ones (whether mental or physical), and various other outside circumstances. Sadly, the world we live in is not in a very happiness-promoting state.

At the church I attended in my young to middle adulthood, we had a pastor who would look at the congregation from his pulpit and intone, "In case you haven't noticed, folks, this is not heaven." No one ever contradicted him because we knew it was true. There wasn't a person in the room who didn't have some kind of problem or fear.

The truth is that we all live on a fallen planet that is suffering from millennia of sin and its associated conditions of pain, hunger, wars, disease, greed, lust, evil, injury, broken relationships, cruelty, neglect, poverty, need, and every other symptom of lack of love one can imagine. I have always been blessed by loving relationships, but, just like everybody else in a sin-soaked world, I have had problems with disease, pain, money problems, loss of loved ones, sorrows over loved ones who are hurting, painful relationships, forced painful decisions, loss of beloved friends, and even pets. So I can't say I am a happy old lady because I've had a perfect life.

And then comes old age, when I think the majority of those people who are not happy become unhappy. Problems encountered or suffered when one is younger, at least, have a chance of going away. We recover, or get over, or outgrow, or heal, and things get better. But with aging, it's just bound to get worse! And what's more, aging is not an elective procedure. Everybody who lives long enough is going to age, no exceptions other than dying, and most people do not see death as a preferable situation.

I read in a book on the subject of aging that old people tend not to like change, and the reason is that the changes are rarely for the better. They are usually an undesired change. Old people often move out of their beloved homes because they can no longer handle stairs, the yard work, or the housework, and move into a smaller, one-level house with a patio and a very small green space. And it is usually a forced change! One's children start interfering with their parents' lives for the parents' own good, and that may be true, but it is still unwelcome. Sometimes we oldies make the decision on our own, out of good sense, but still resentfully.

I recently made the decision to stop driving at night, and while it was a safe and correct decision, I still didn't like it. It reflected a minimalizing of my freedom. Changes for aging people are rarely for the better. That's just the way it is.

Of course, all these types of changes are the circumstances we face as we grow older, and remembering that circumstances are part of God's sanctification process puts a whole different spin on the situation. The circumstances are God's, remember? It is only the response that is mine. So the whole thing becomes a spiritual issue, and that's when we get to realize that all issues brought up by circumstances are spiritual. Sanctification—becoming like Jesus—is definitely part of the aging process!

Maybe circumstances and sanctification are part of the happy old lady thing. As circumstances have been engineered by God, I've learned some important spiritual truths that have really helped with the sanctification process. I think I mentioned that temper tantrums will not be a part of heaven because there will be no sin in heaven because everybody there will be just like Jesus, and Jesus was totally sinless.

Truths I've come to believe along the way have eliminated some of the behaviors associated with childishness. Because I believe that God is completely, sovereignly in control of heaven and earth, and I also believe that God, as my heavenly Father, loves me unconditionally and will never leave me or desert me, I don't have to be afraid. Yes, eventually, I will die, and I might even get hurt along the way, but the part of me that will live forever is totally safe. My body will die, but my soul and spirit are immortal. Jesus certainly got hurt, and He died on the cross, but after three days, He rose from the dead. His followers will experience death and resurrection like their Master. So I am secure, and I am not afraid of death.

I have also come to believe that God's sovereign will is good, and acceptable, and perfect. If I believe that God is in control of my life and death, I can trust that whatever God's will is for my life is also good, acceptable, and perfect. I don't have to worry about my future, the aging process, disease, or death because I am trusting in God's will for my life.

In John 10, Jesus promises that His sheep, those who come in through the Door of the sheepfold, which is Jesus Himself, will have and enjoy life, and have it in abundance, to the full, till it overflows. What more could anyone want? I am safe, I am secure, and I am promised a happy life. How could I ask for anything more?

I am truly a happy old lady. And it is my greatest desire that all of my Christian sisters and brothers have and live in this same amazing God-given safety, security, and happiness that I experience daily. There is no secret about it. God does not give this gift to just a select few who know the password or possess the key to the Happiness Gate. John 10 is for every single one of the sheep of His pasture—me, you, everyone who believes that Jesus died for their sin and rose again to live within them.

Read again John 3:16:

> For God so loved the world, that He gave His only begotten Son, that Whosoever (that's you and me!) believes

> in Him should not perish, but have eternal life.

Then as a believer, read John 10. Believe it. Receive it as yours, and it is.

God loves every human being He has created, and He wants to have a relationship with them and bless them. The only requirement is to believe it—with the kind of belief that transforms your thinking, your emotions, and your actions. Real belief. Not the kind the demons have. Scripture says that even demons believe in God…and shudder! It makes no positive difference to their lives.

There is an old story about a man who made his living walking across Niagara Falls on a tightrope. He charged people to come and watch him do it, and many came. One day, the man asked the crowd this question: "How many of you believe I can walk safely across this waterfall?" Everyone there raised their hands. Then the man asked, "How many of you believe that I can push a person in this wheelbarrow across safely?" Again, everyone in the crowd raised their hands.

"Who's first?"

Not a single person raised a hand. No one believed enough to bet their life on the man and the wheelbarrow.

What I'm asking you to do requires the same kind of faith—faith that makes a difference in your life—but if I'm wrong, it won't kill you. You have nothing to lose, and a life of heaven right here on earth if I'm right. And I am! I know that bccausc I didn't make all this up. It's from God, and He wrote it all down for you to read yourself in His Good Book.

And by the way, I'm not the only happy old lady in the world. There are thousands of others—and happy old men too. You can tell them by looking at their happy faces and shining eyes. God gives all His children the blessing of happiness, but not all of them believe that and receive it. That is a real shame, and it is also, in my opinion, a sin. We are called to give glory to God, and what better way to give glory to God than to exhibit the joy and happiness that He blesses us with?

I think, and it is possibly just my opinion, but I think every Christian has a sacred obligation, a duty even, to showcase and to express the blessing of joy and happiness we have been given, just because we belong to Jesus and will get to spend eternity with Him.

As I look back on my life, and see where I've been, what I've experienced, how blessed I've been, and what is promised for my future, I am not at all surprised that I am happy. What surprises me is that every believer is not!

# *About the Author*

Rita Weber was born into a military family in March of 1945 and lived in several parts of the United States and in Japan during her childhood. Her family settled in Albuquerque, New Mexico, just before her high school years, and after graduation, Rita attended the University of New Mexico, majoring in biology. At eleven years old, Rita gave her life to the Lord Jesus Christ and has greatly enjoyed her experience of the goodness of God to her right up until now, in her eightieth year. Rita is a widow and has two adult children—a daughter and a son—and two grandchildren. She considers herself very blessed and looks forward to spending eternity in heaven.

www.ingramcontent.com/pod-product-compliance
Ingram Content Group UK Ltd.
Pitfield, Milton Keynes, MK11 3LW, UK
UKHW040248231125
9120UKWH00001B/67

9 798897 854288